COWBOY CARVING

with

CLEVE TAYLOR

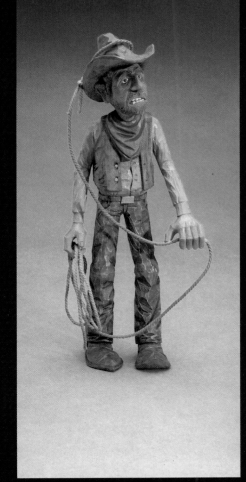

D1605067

77 Lower Valley Road, Atglen, PA 19310

ACKNOWLEDGEMENTS

There are a few very special people in my life that deserve much of the credit for whatever success I have or will have as a wood-carver. They have enhanced my efforts with support and encouragement, and for that I am very grateful. My sincere thanks to the following:

Members of the Idaho Woodcarvers Guild who were so gracious with their compliments even when my characters had no discernible eyes or six fingers per hand, and especially to Kathleen, Ted and Larry who always have the time to listen, consult and advise.

My mother, father, brother, and sister for being so caring, loving and supportive of all that I am and for teaching and assisting me with making a lot of quilts.

My wife, Sandy, bless her heart, for so many wonderful and beautiful qualities, but especially for not fussing about the wood chips in the carpet and the paint on my clothes. Of course I have to vacuum, but she does the laundry. And to our son Arn, who actually has mowed the lawn so I could carve.

Thanks again folks!

Copyright © 1994 by Cleve Taylor
Library of Congress Catalog Number: 94-66200

Printed in Hong Kong
ISBN: 0-88740-641-6

We are interested in hearing from authors
with book ideas on related topics.

Published by Schiffer Publishing Ltd.
77 Lower Valley Road
Atglen, PA 19310
Please write for a free catalog. This book may
be purchased from the publisher.
Please include $2.95 postage.
Try your bookstore first.

CONTENTS

ACKNOWLEDGEMENTS.....2

INTRODUCTION.....3

THE COWBOY PATTERN.....4

CARVING THE COWBOY.....6

PAINTING THE COWBOY.....47

THE GALLERY.....52

INTRODUCTION

The two most frequently asked questions of my wife and I when we display my cowboys at art shows are, (1) "What kind of wood do you use?" and (2) "How long does it take you to carve a figure?" Several years ago in an attempt to add a little humor to my rather bland personality, I had T-shirts printed with the answers to these questions. Now when someone asks "What kind of wood?", I point to line one on my shirt that reads "Basswood". If the second question is asked, I point to line two that reads "Depends - sometimes 4, some-times 40". The third most frequently asked question is something to the effect of "Why is there no horse, or cow, manure in the scene?" Well, I couldn't bring myself to print "Not in good taste" on the shirts since those folks that didn't ask the question would probably assume that it was my way of exposing the true nature of myself and I wasn't about to answer that there's none on the scenes because I was so full of it and there's none left over to use. So I created the "Pooper Scooper" as a permanent part of my display so that all I have to do is point to him when asked that third question.

THE COWBOY

Tools:

Here are the tools you will need for this project:
I use a Kevlar carving glove impervious to knife cuts, a series of bench knives, a Foredom or Dremel rotary power tool with a Kutzall burr, and a band saw. The gouges I use are a 1/4" #9 gouge, 1/2" #3 fishtail gouge, three different size V tools (1/4", 1/8", and a micro 2 mm or 1/16" V gouge), a 3/16" deep gouge, a 1/8" #5, and a 1/2" #7, 3/32" deep gouge (deep gouges are also called veiners).

I hope you enjoy carving your cowboys as much as I do mine.

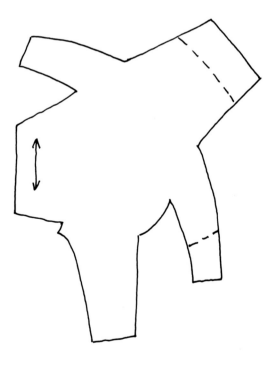

PATTERN

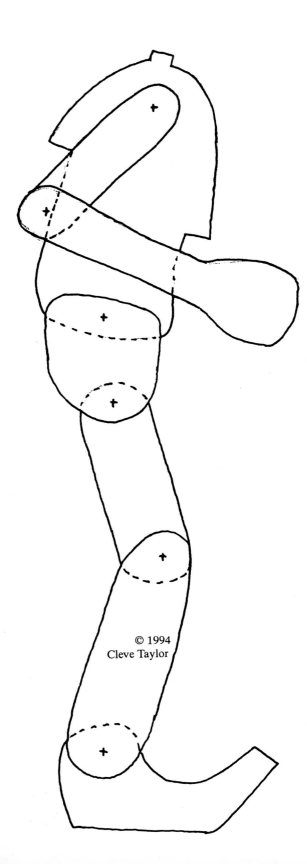

© 1994
Cleve Taylor

Flexible Cowboy

If you examine the line drawings we have included for your use in replicating my carvings, it will be obvious to you that I can't draw. In fact, I have to complete a carving first and then attempt to draw what I've done. My mental images are three dimensional explaining, at least to me, why I can create my images in three dimensions but not on a two dimensional plane. It became necessary several years ago that I develop something that would allow me to overcome this deficiency if I was to grow as a carver and produce my own ideas rather than continue to replicate other's work.

The device that evolved from my efforts is the flexible contraption I lovingly refer to as "Bojangles". This is a copyrighted item. If you would like to purchase a "Bojangles," complete with detailed instructions on how to use it, the cost is $20.00 plus $2.00 for postage. Until at least 2005, I may be reached at 11052 Sandhurst, Boise, ID 83709. I aslo have flexible patterns for a horse and a golfer for the same price. You may also order any blank in this book for $23.00 and $2.00 postage.

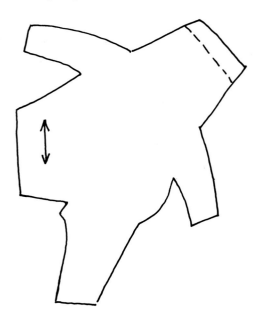

CARVING THE COWBOY

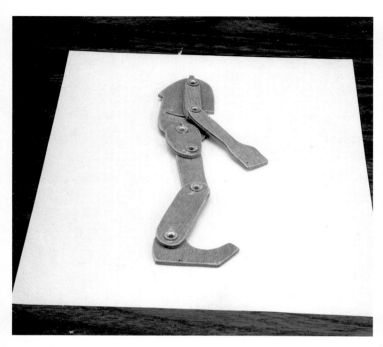

Place Bojangles on your paper (or directly on the wood if you don't want to keep a copy of the resulting pattern for future use) and position the arm and leg for the pose you desire for the left side of the cowboy.

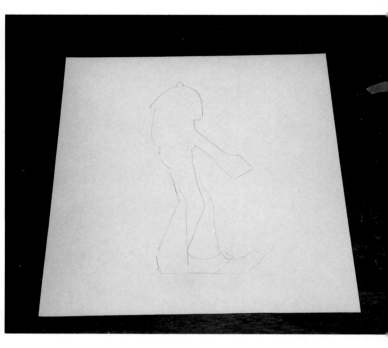

Position the arm and leg for the pose you desire for the right side of the cowboy. Keep the upper body aligned with the left side pattern we drew previously.

Trace the outline of the left side of the body.

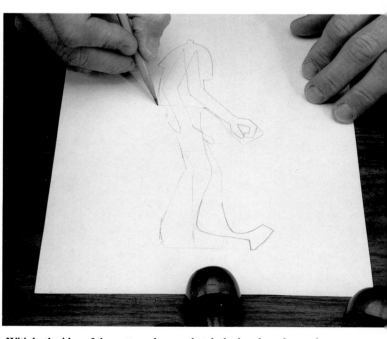

With both sides of the pattern drawn, sketch the hands and arms in. We have determined we will have one boot turned up and the other boot with the toe on the ground. Add lines for a vest as well.

Take a darker pencil and sketch around the perimeter of the pattern to help make sense of all the lines. Once you have a nice, dark perimeter, transfer the pattern to a block of bass wood 3" thick x 3 1/2" x 8 1/2".

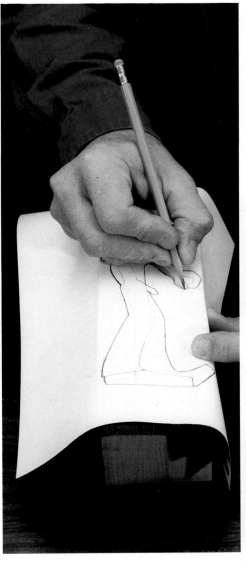

Transfer the pattern to the wood using a piece of carbon paper and tracing the pattern with a pencil. I know what you're thinking but that is a thumb!

Rather than using a pattern from paper for the head, I'm using a permanent pattern piece made by sawing a 1/8" thick slice from a previous cut out of the head. Most of my heads are cut from 2" thick basswood, giving me a narrower hat brim as an outcome.

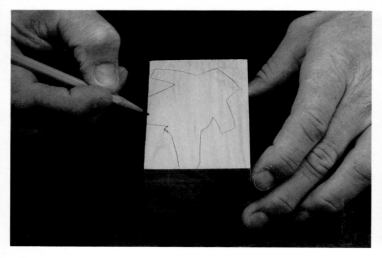

The direction of the grain should be parallel to this plane of the face I am pointing to.

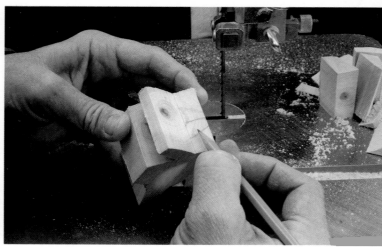

Sketch in the crown of the hat.

Cut out the head on the band saw.

Cut out the neck and the crown of the hat.

Draw in a center line on the cut out head and sketch in the neck about 1/2" wide.

Now cut out the body. Plan your cuts to minimize the number of back outs for the blade.

Draw a center line down the front of the figure. Sketch in the front view of the figure around that center line.

Continue removing excess wood from the front view.

Cut out the front view of the figure, removing as much excess wood as possible.

Sketch the shape of the hat brim on the top ...

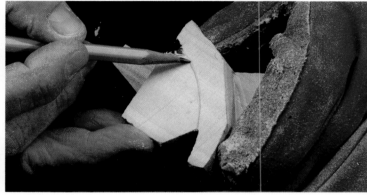

... and side of the head.

Cut out the head below the hat brim using a Foredom with a Kutzall carbide burr and a leather glove on the holding hand. Cut about 1/4" deep with the Kutzall. There are some purists out there who will disagree with using power tools to remove wood, but I've also used worms on a fly rod and believe whatever works you ought to use.

The cut down sides.

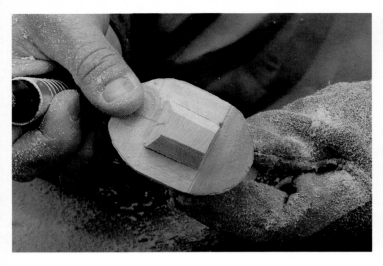

Now follow the brim of the hat, removing excess material.

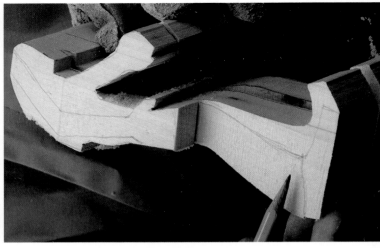

Moving to the body, we have to sketch in the arm and legs on both sides of the body.

Cut the inside of the hat brim, cutting about 1/4" all around. Be aware you don't want to cut through the brim of the hat.

We'll want to cut the least fragile parts first. Since the arms have a tendency to break off at the shoulder we'll start with the legs.

This is how the hat should look at this point.

Removing wood from underneath the arm.

Proceed to the arms, remove the excess wood of the left arm from the right side with the Foredom.

Sketch in the bandanna, front ...

We'll start on the right side removing unwanted wood.

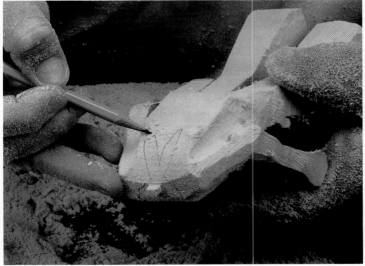

... and back.

Now remove excess wood to the level of the shirt, defining the bandanna.

Remove wood to the sketch lines.

You may want to round down the arms, legs and trunk at this time, removing the excess thumb material as you go.

Sketch in the boots. Draw a center line down the base of the boot and sketch in the base of the boots like so.

Sketch in the hands on the front view and on both sides.

Change to a smaller 1/8" Kutzall burr in the Foredom tool, or to save time, use a separate tool with the 1/8" burr so you don't have to change them. Begin rounding the hand.

With a small Kutzall, cut in some of the larger details like the overlap of the pants cuff above the boot.

Drill the hole for the eventual cup of the fingers.

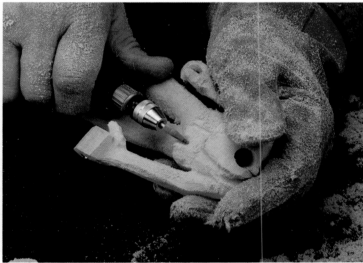

Dress up any rough spots and cut in the front of the vest. Cut down the material between the open edges of the vest for the shirt beneath.

The rounded hand. The other hand is cut in a similar manner.

The last thing to do to the blank is to drill a 1/2" hole for the neck to fit into. This hole is carefully drilled to a depth of about an inch. If you want the head cocked to one side, drill the hole inclined to the center line of the body.

It is time to start carving the details on the head. Begin with the 1/2" fishtail gouge and cut from the bottom of the head towards the hat brim, shaping the head so that, viewed from the bottom, it will appear oval.

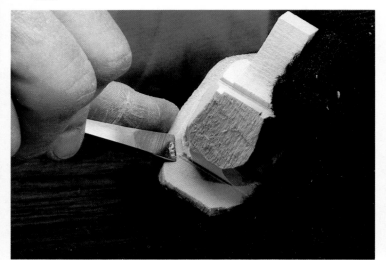

Put a stop cut along the hat brim ...

... and along the back of the head at the hat brim.

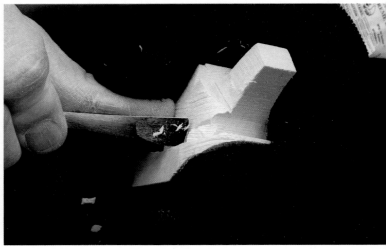

But cut from the hat brim towards the neck.

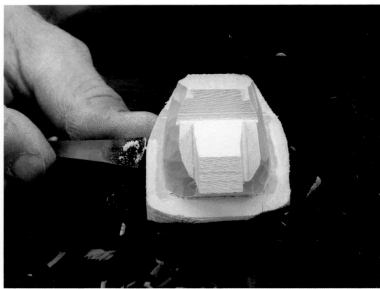

Remembering that the grain is running vertically along the front of the face, cut with the grain to avoid chipping. See the oval shape created once the head is shaped.

Now draw in the ear. First we put a point in that divides the neck in halves and then a point along the bottom of the hat brim that divides the head into equal halves. Connect those two dots with a line.

Depending on how large you want the ear to be, draw in a line representing the back of the ear. Repeat on the other side of the head.

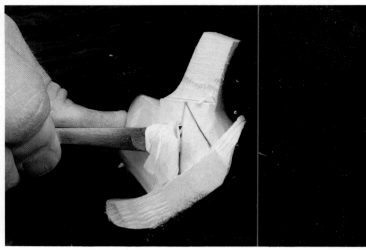

We will remove wood from the head to the front of the ear.

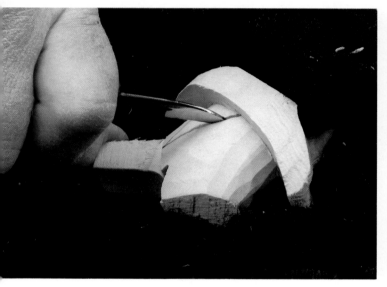

Using a bench knife, score the line along the front and back of the ear to a depth of about 3/16". The depth depends on how far you want the ear to protrude from the head.

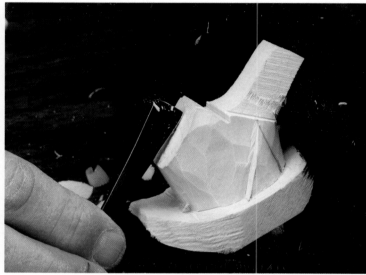

These cuts should be made perpendicular to the front of the ear.

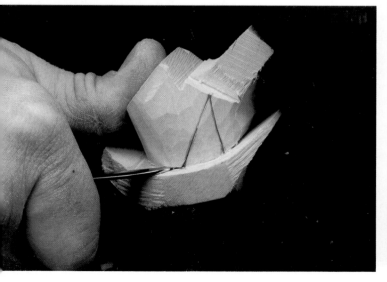

Score also along the hat brim.

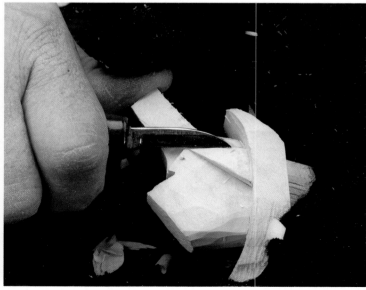

Remove the wood from the back of the ear.

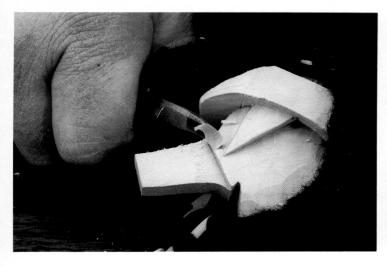

Round off the back of the head to the ear.

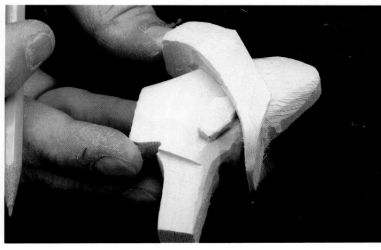

The ear with the notches removed.

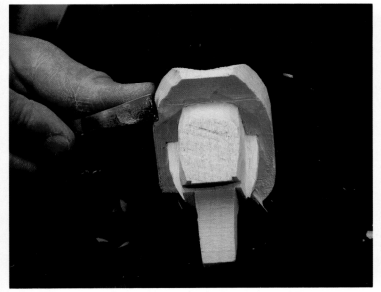

Check for symmetry, making sure both ears protrude the same distance from the sides of the head.

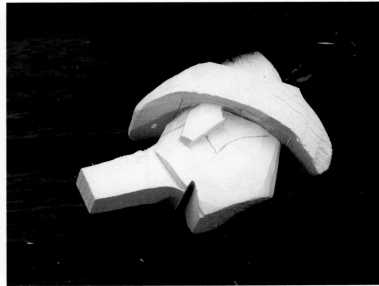

Draw in the sideburns and the hairline at the back of the head.

Draw in three guide lines along the sharp corners of the ear wedges and notch out the triangles to round the ears.

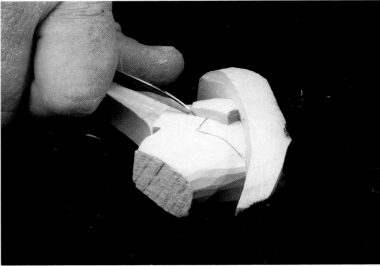

Score along these lines to a depth of about 1/16".

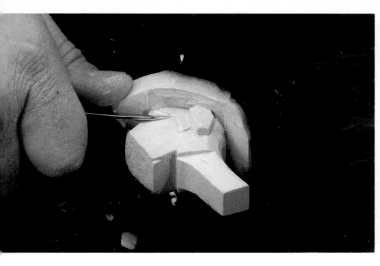

Remove 1/16" of wood along the front of the hairline to the score cut.

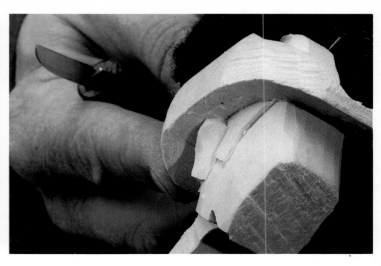

Add a little character to the ear by notching it to give the ear a floppy shape as viewed from the front.

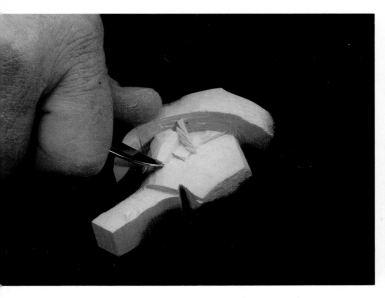

Now we will finish the ear before going on to any other details. First take the knife and shave off at about a 45 degree angle down to the outside surface of the sideburns first. Undercut the ear where the ear meets the sideburns.

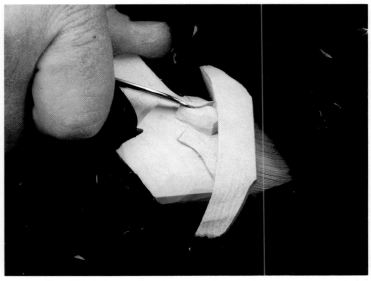

We can also do the same thing in the side view and shape up the ear lobe by removing it's sharp corners.

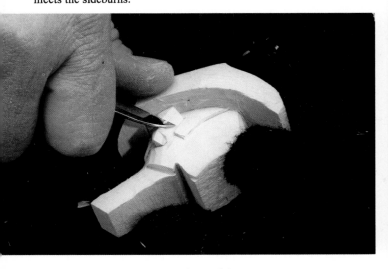

Clip off the sharp corner at the front of the ear.

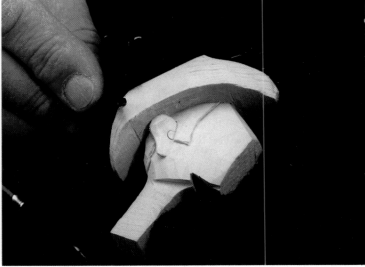

Using a 3/16" deep gouge, push straight down into the ear to score the tragus to a depth of about 1/8".

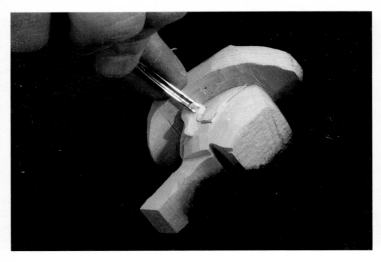

Switching to the 3/32" deep gouge, remove wood from the inside of the ear to the depth of the tragus cut.

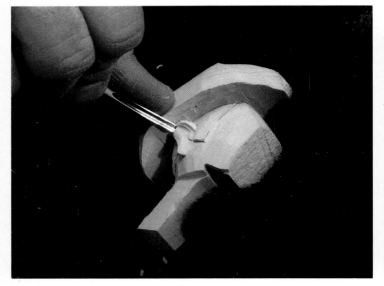

Using the 1/8" #5 gouge, round off the sharp edges left by the 3/32" gouge.

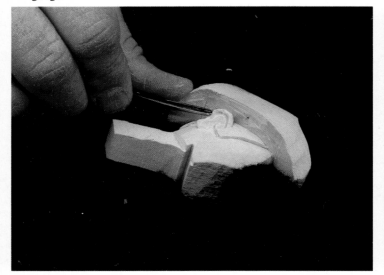

Using the smallest veiner you have, put in a trough around the inside of the back edge of the ear.

Both ears are complete. I don't generally complete one ear and then move to the other side. I make a cut on one ear, move immediately to the other ear, making an identical cut. This way the ears come out more symmetrically.

Draw in a center line down the face.

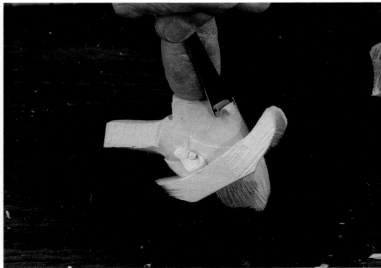

Using the 1/2" fishtail gouge, we'll round off the face from the leading edge of the sideburns to the center line of the head.

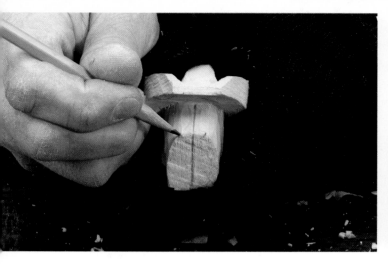

This ridge represents the tip of the nose. Determine and mark the width of the nose you want.

Draw a guide line from along the chin, parallel with the front of the ear, up the side of the head.

Mark a point that is about 3/32" below the hat brim along the center line of the head. This represents the intersection of the eyebrows and the center of the nose. Connect the dots, forming the triangular outline of the nose.

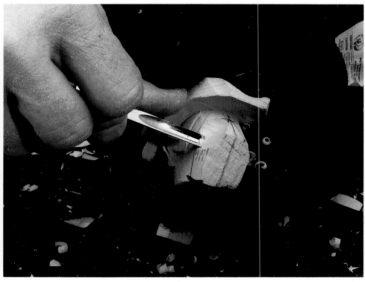

Using the 1/4" #9 gouge, cut perpendicular to the center line of the face ...

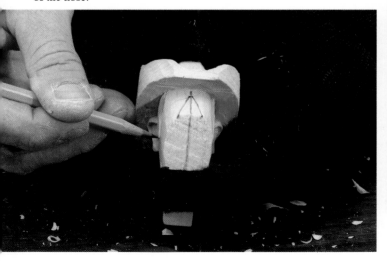

Now then, connect this dot intersecting the nose and eyebrows with the bottom of the ear lobe like this.

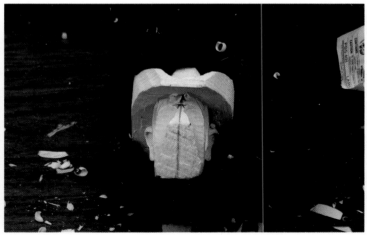

... removing excess wood from the area of the eye, following the lines of the nose and the line down the side of the face to the chin. Using a 1/4" #9 gouge, begin cutting from the line on the side of the face and then sweeping outwards to meet the edge of the nose. It should look like this when both sides are finished.

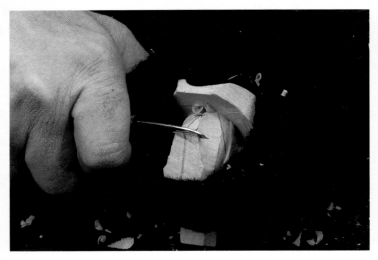

Cut in along the base of the nose with a bench knife and remove wood from beneath that cut.

The rounded face.

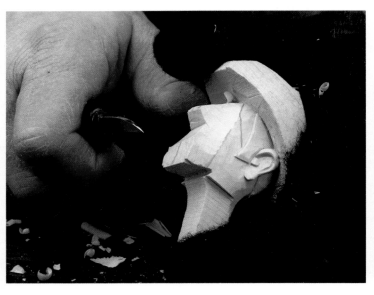

This will give you the profile of the nose.

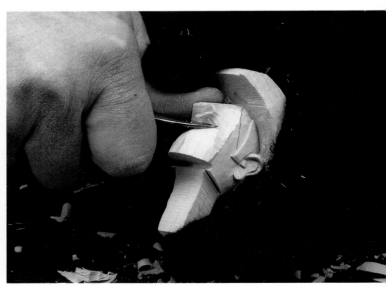

Begin to shape the nose, angling the cut from the center line angled towards the top of the ear.

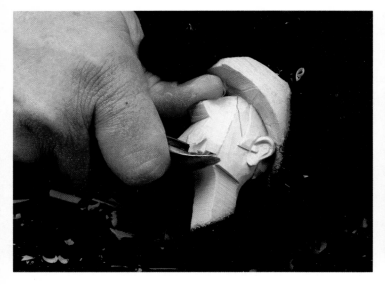

Redraw the center line underneath the nose and remove the sharp edges of the mouth and chin area.

Cut the bridge of the nose by removing a triangular notch which viewed from the sides gives the profile of a nose that has been kicked by many horses or slapped by many cowgirls.

Round the sides of the nose angling the blade from the center line outwards.

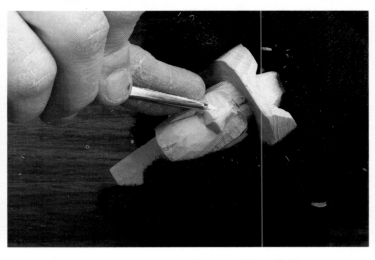

Using the 3/16" deep gouge, from the bottom of the smile line cut at the nostril of the nose, remove wood along the side of the nose up to the top of the nose.

Draw in the smile line and, using the 1/8" V tool, begin cutting this smile line into the face.

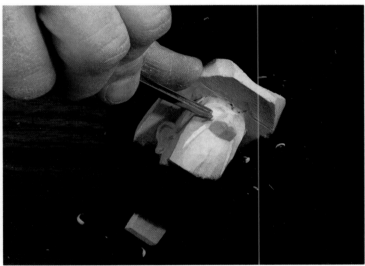

Using the same 3/16" gouge, form a deeper eye socket.

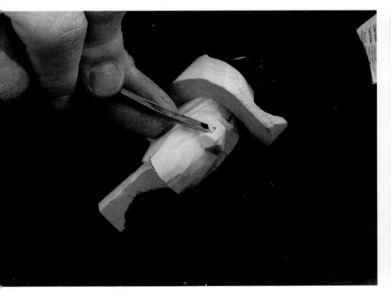

Continue cutting into the nose.

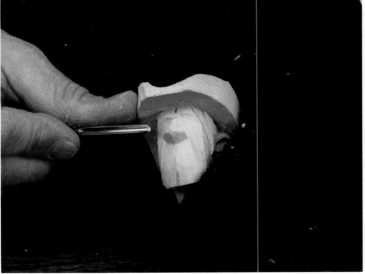

It is important that the left and right sockets are identical.

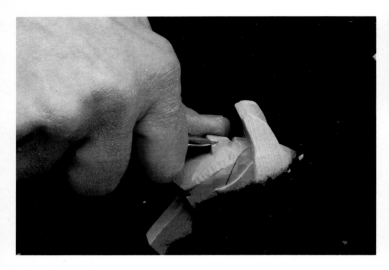

Using your knife tip, form the nostril by gouging out as shown.

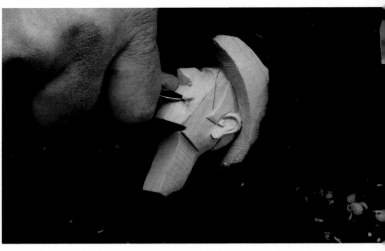

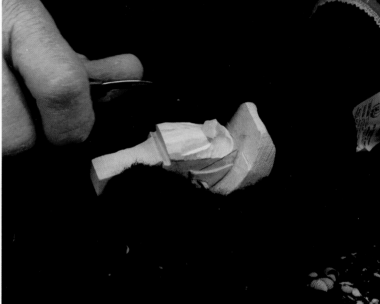

Remove the ridge of wood along the smile line to the nostril.

Take the knife tip and clip off the end of the nostril like so.

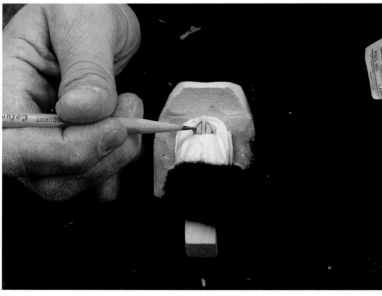

Draw in the nostrils.

Take a smaller detail knife and cut along the lines in the nostril.

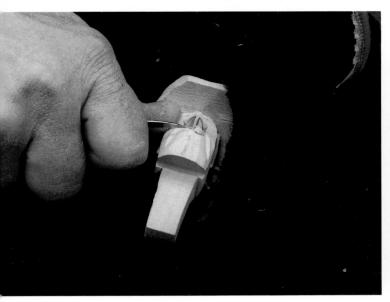

Then make a stop cut at the base of the nose and flip that little triangular piece out to create the nostril.

Round off the sharp tip of the nose.

Draw in the eye. Draw an oval in, dropping the outside corner lower on the face than the inside corner. This makes the cowboy look more Caucasian than oriental and it will make his face appear to be weathered, tired and haggard. Attempt to duplicate the eye on the other side of the face.

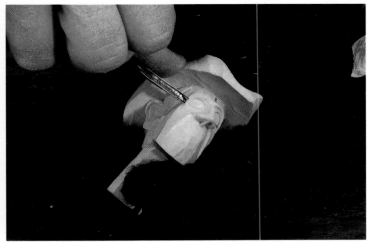

It pays to know that very few people have identically shaped eyes. Using a medium sized V tool, cut in the oval. I start with the cowboys right eye first since it has to be carved in a more awkward position than the other eye. Cut along the top outer edge first. Repeat on the lower edge.

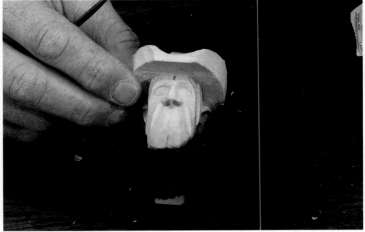

Now we have two small footballs, the beginnings of eyes.

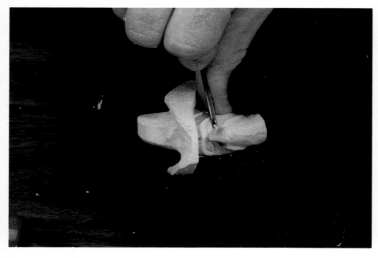

Remove the sharp edge created by the V tool along the lower edge of the eye.

Draw in the top and bottom eyelid along the trough formed by the V tool.

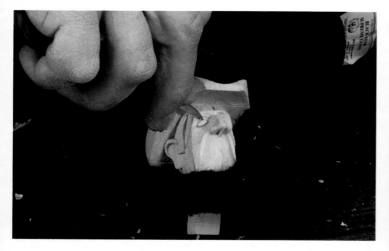

Slip the edge of your detail knife in along the bottom of the top eyelid at the inside corner of the eye about 1/16" deep. Pull the knife tip along the bottom of the eyebrow to the outside corner of the eye. Repeat along the bottom of the eye.

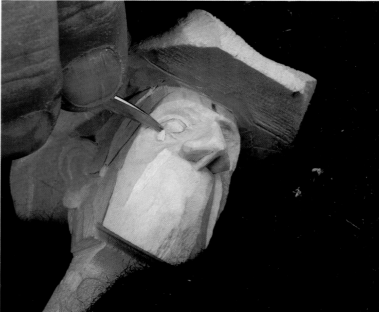

With the knife tip flip out the little triangle along the inside and outside corners of the eyes. Round off the eyeball between the two eyelids with the detail knife.

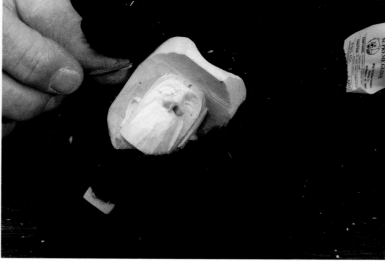

The rounded eyes.

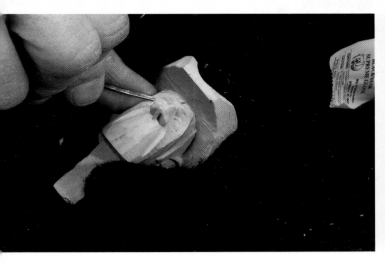

Use the smallest V tool to extend the upper eye lid beyond the edge of the eye ...

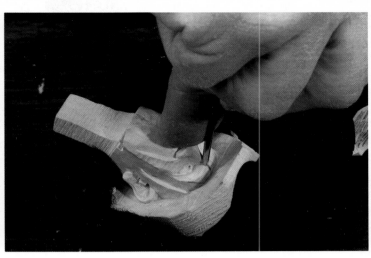

It is time to form the eyebrows. Take the 3/16" deep gouge and, beginning at the top of the nose, carve along the center line of the face up to the hat brim.

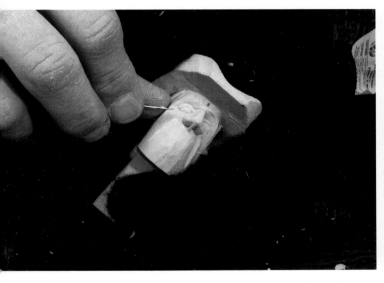

... and notch out beneath the extended lid with the detailing knife.

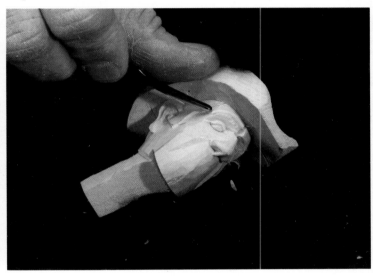

Slightly above the outside corner of the eye, cut a groove in along the top of the eyebrow, meeting at the center line.

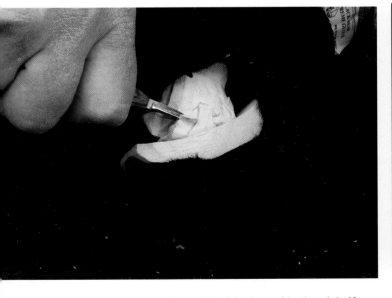

Indent the temple area on either side of the face with a bench knife.

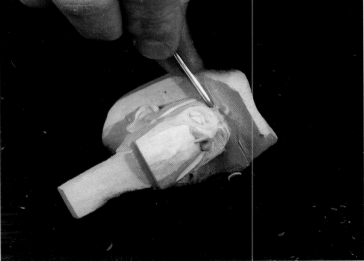

Using the 1/8" gouge, clean the forehead from the top of the eyebrow to the bottom of the hat brim.

Here's how the eyebrows and forehead should appear.

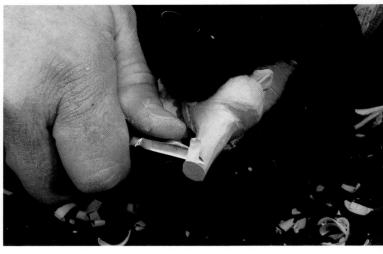

Continue down the jaw line, rounding out the neck.

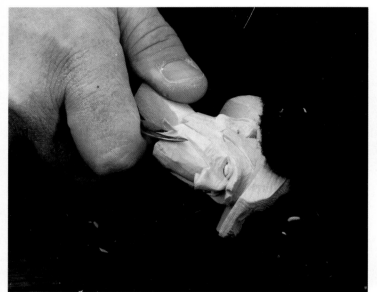

Round off the chin.

Check the diameter of the neck to make sure it will fit to the body while you are rounding down the neck.

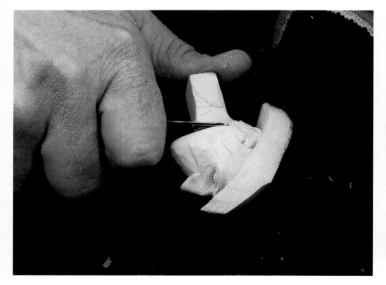

As we continue to round out the chin, round back to the ear to form the jaw line.

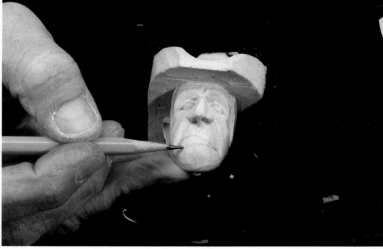

Because of the predicament we are going to put this cowboy in, we want to put some expression on his mouth to indicate frustration. We'll put a sag in the corners and a grimace on one side.

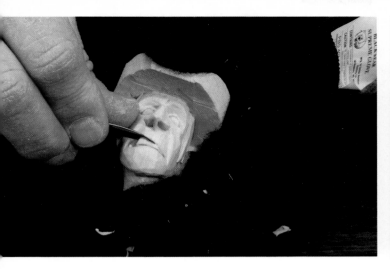

With a detail knife, score the outline of the mouth about 1/16" deep. Remove the wood between the lips.

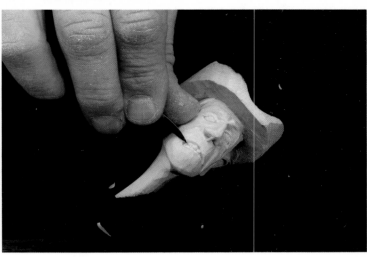

Our objective is to make these teeth look rough because dentists and orthodontists are hard to come by on the open range.

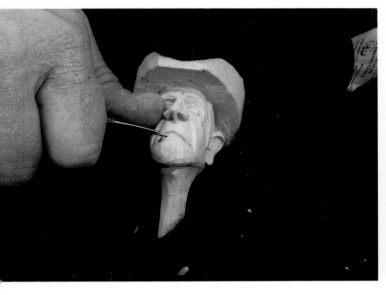

Score a horizontal line separating the top teeth from the bottom teeth. Start separating the teeth with the tip of the knife. Make the teeth large for the mouth to give the cowboy a less sweet look.

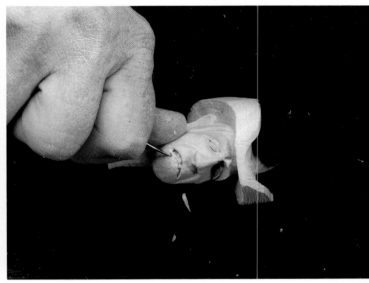

When you get the teeth where you want them, round off the lower lip with a knife tip.

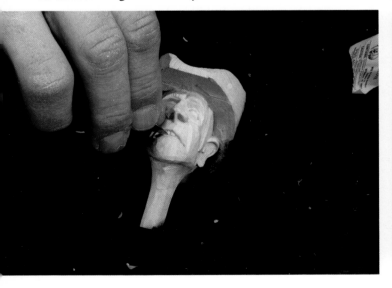

Round off the bottom corners of the teeth.

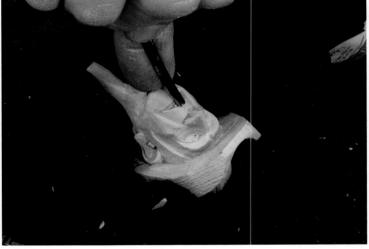

With the 3/16" deep gouge strike a groove from the top lip to the septum.

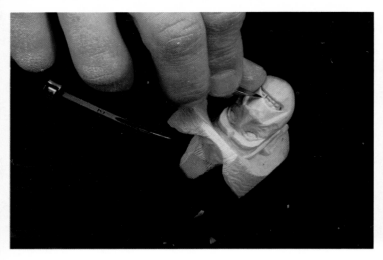

From either side of that "angels dimple" round off the top lip. As the story goes, when babies are born they have all the knowledge of heaven. An angel gently rests a finger across their lips so they can never tell, forming the angel's dimple.

Accent the smile line along the grimacing side of the face with a bench knife tip, undercutting the length of the smile line.

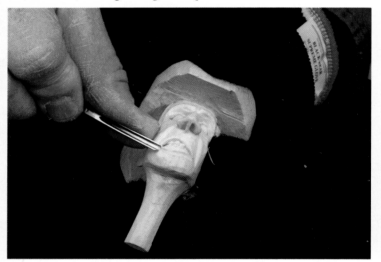

Using the 3/16" deep gouge, start at the corner of the lips and run a groove across the lower part of the lower lip to define it.

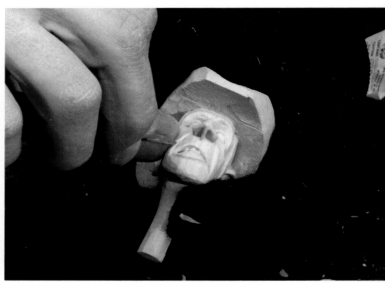

Remove a strip of wood from the smile line.

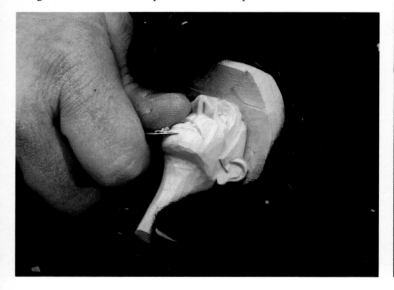

Use the detail knife to remove the wood along the chin to the depth of that lip forming groove.

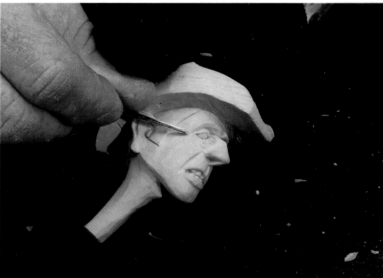

With the 1/16" V tool add some crows feet lines to the outside corners of the eyes on both sides.

Using the small V tool, form some lines indicative of bags under the eyes.

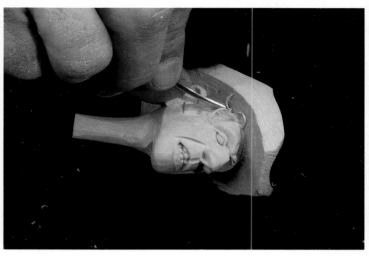

Using the same V tool, carve in the semblance of hair with very crooked and uneven lines. The objective is to show hair that has not seen a comb or been brushed in many days.

With the small V tool, form the hair of the eyebrows.

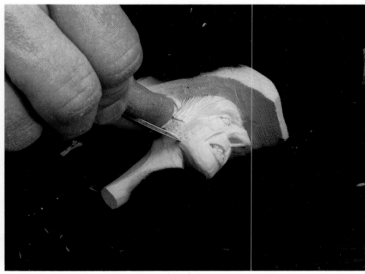

I use this 1/16" V tool to flip out small triangles of wood to give this guy a couple days worth of beard growth. Other tools which would give the same effect are nails and shallow gouges. Old Steve Prescott down in Fort Worth uses an engraving tool.

Continuing with the small 1/16" V tool, add some worry lines to the forehead as well.

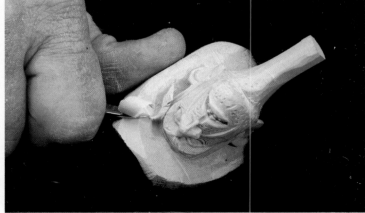

Starting in the middle of the front of the hat, remove the hat's sharp corners with a bench knife. It's important to cut from the front of the head to the back on the underside of the hat brim and from the back of the head to the front on the top side of the hat brim.

Using the 1/4" #9 gouge, shape the inside of the hat brim.

The back of the crown is cut in the other direction from the crown to the brim.

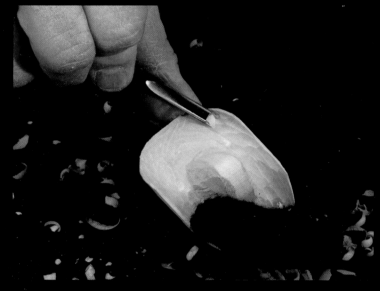

The inside brim of the hat is carved. Be careful not to get too thin.

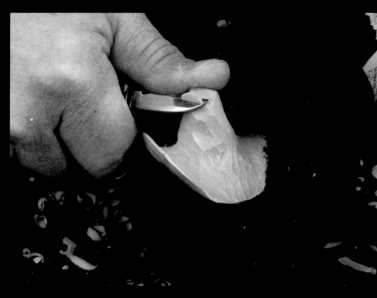

Rough up the crown with some large cuts to indicate many years hard use as a fly swatter and water tank.

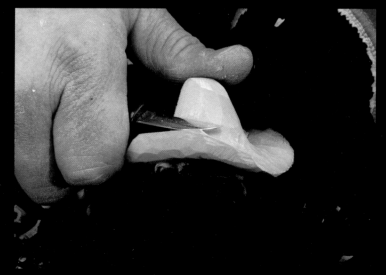

The front part of the hat brim needs to be cut from the hat brim to the top of the crown in this direction.

Finally, we will trim the edge of the brim of the hat.

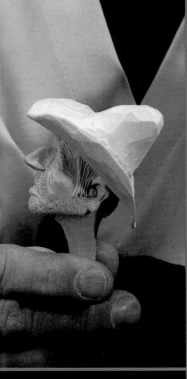

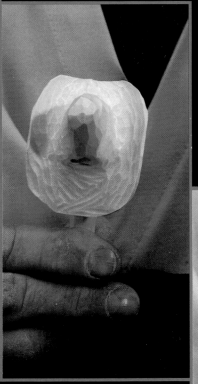

Here is the carved head.

It's time to work on the body. Start by using a bench knife to round the body and remove saw marks and other unwanted material.

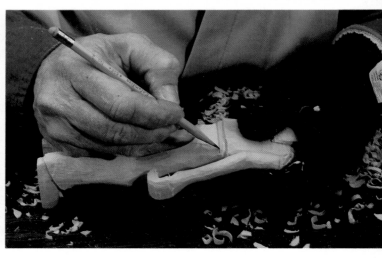

While we're rounding this is a good time to cut in the bottom of the shirt. Draw in the location of the shirt and ...

At the major intersections of body parts I use the large V tool to begin the rounding process. For other areas, a bench knife works fine.

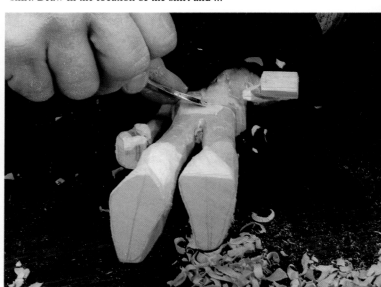

... cut it in with a V tool.

Wherever there is a grain change, use a gouge to remove the burrs.

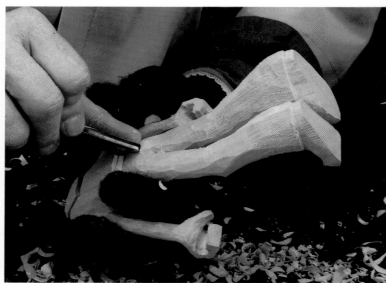

To work around the inside of the legs, use the large V tool.

Use the large V tool to cut in the bottom of each pant leg.

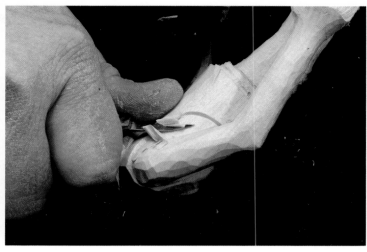

Using the detail knife and small gouges when necessary, shave the shirt to the bottom of the outline of the armhole.

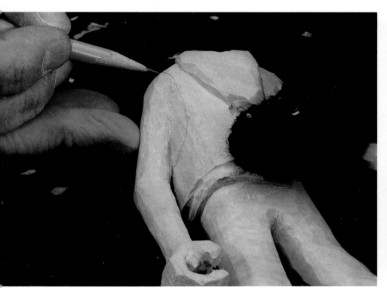

Moving on to the vest, first sketch in the arm holes.

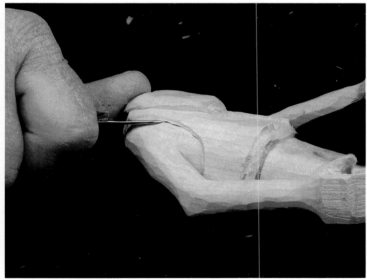

Undercut the vest with the detail knife to make it appear as if the shirt and body actually continue beneath the vest.

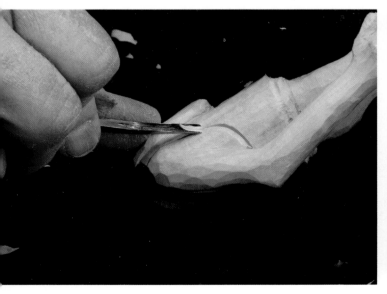

Use a medium V tool and cut in the line of the arm hole.

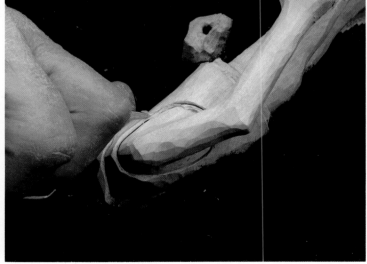

Come back now at about a 45 degree angle to the first cut and remove the excess material. This creates the appearance you are looking for.

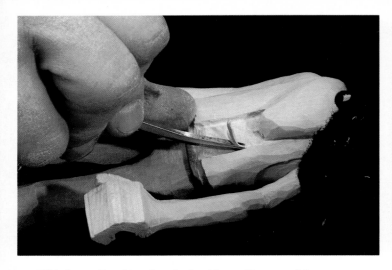

With the medium V tool cut in the sides and bottom of the vest.

Undercut the front of the vest as we did with the armholes, first using a cut along the surface of the shirt front.

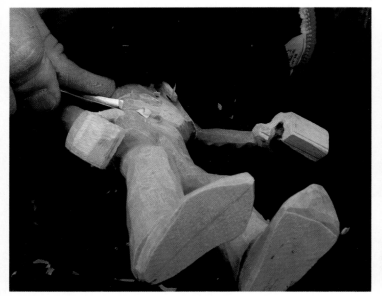

Using the detail knife and the 1/4" V gouge on the shirt that extends from underneath the vest. Use the same tools to cut in the bottom of the vest.

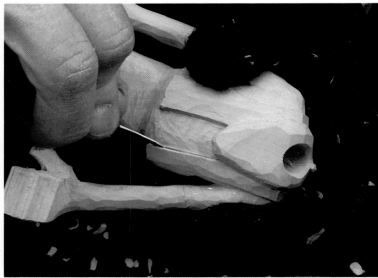

Now make an oblique cut to it and pop out the extra wood.

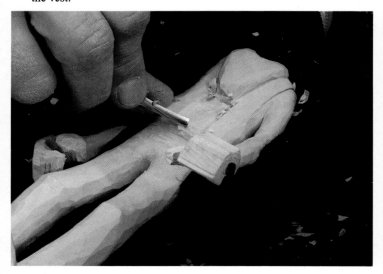

Clean off the shirt front between the lapels of the vest with the 1/4" #5 gouge.

The vest has been undercut.

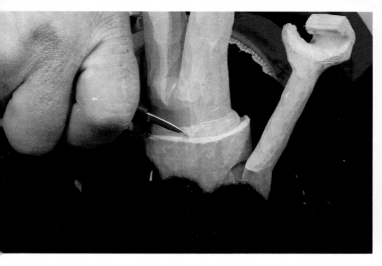

Undercut the vest along the bottom edge with the bench knife in a similar fashion to the arm holes and the front of the vest.

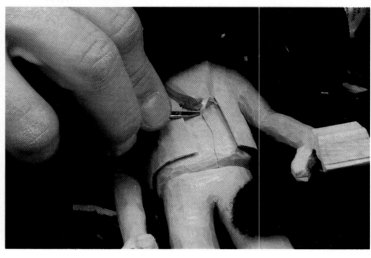

To make the front of the shirt take a detail knife and make an irregular cut down the front of the shirt about 1/32" deep. Use the detail knife again to relieve the right side of the shirt to the depth of the scored line. If you are carving a cowgirl, or a cowboy wearing cowgirl clothes, you would want to relieve the left side of the shirt since the right side of a woman's blouses overlap the left.

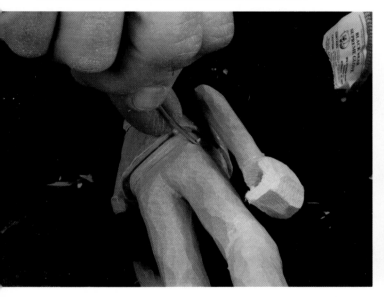

To give the pants some thickness, score around the top of the pants with a 1/16" V tool.

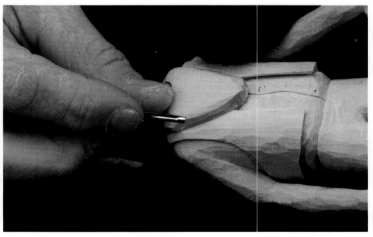

Locate the sites of several buttons along the shirt front. Using the 1/8" gouge, depress the top side of the button and then the bottom side to create the impression of buttons.

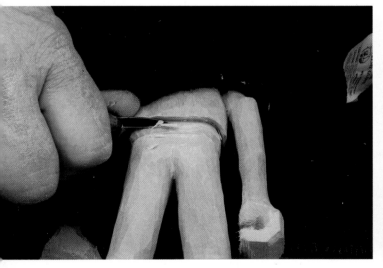

Tuck the shirt tail into the pants using the detail knife, rounding down into the pants to give the bottom of the shirt a billowed, tucked in effect.

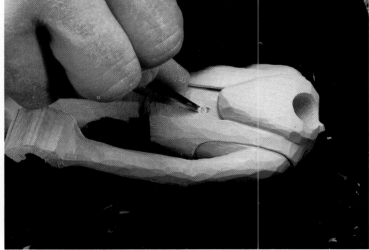

Then using the same gouge relieve the top side and the bottom side to give the buttons depth.

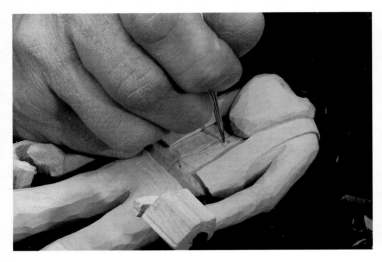

Put in some button holes with a small awl.

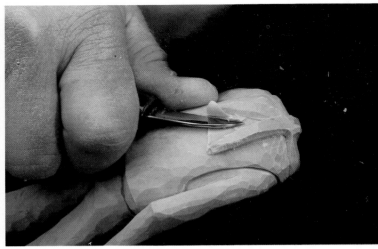

Remove the wood between the tails with a bench knife.

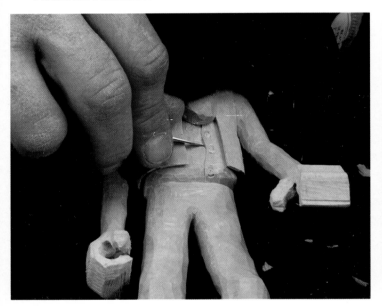

To make the shirt appear bloused, remove some material from the right hand side of the shirt between the buttons.

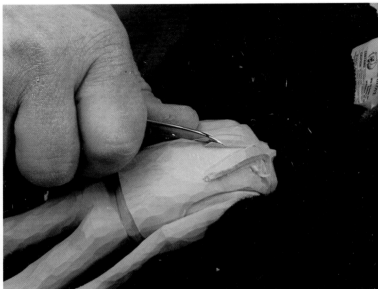

Now round the tails with the bench knife. Let's make one of the tails shorter than the other.

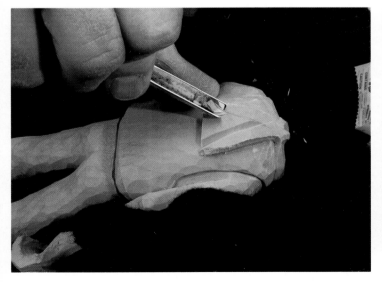

Now we're going to finish off the bandanna. Begin by drawing in the loose ends in the back. Cut these in with a large V tool.

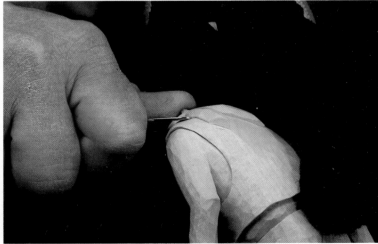

The more undercutting you can do on contiguous surfaces, the more opportunity you can allow for shadows which define the work and produce interesting effects when painted. Undercut all around the bandanna.

Use your large V tool to carve folds into the front of the bandanna. I usually make one complete cut around the neck opening and stagger the cuts from there to the tip.

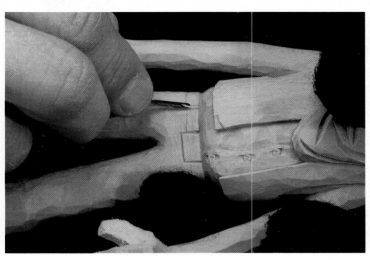

Using the small V tool, start outlining the belt buckle and the belt loops.

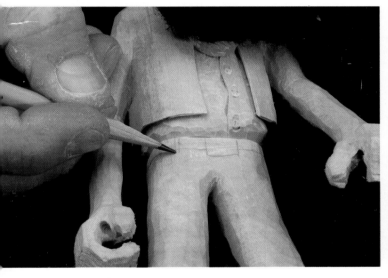

Now let's move to the belt. Draw in a fairly large belt buckle, the belt itself and the belt loops.

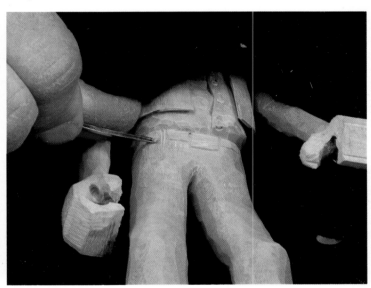

Outline the bottom of the belt itself. Be extremely careful to not run the small V tool over the belt loop.

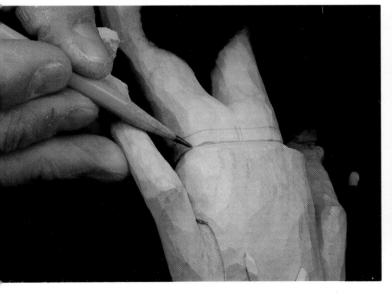

Continue the process all the way around.

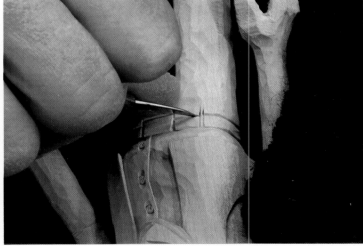

With the tip of your detail knife score a fairly deep cut on either side of the belt loop under the bottom edge of the belt. Again with the detail knife, score a line at the bottom of the belt itself that intersects with the belt loop.

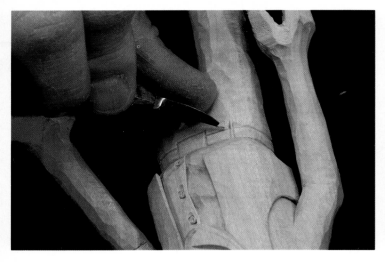

Flick out the little triangle of wood along either side of the scored belt loop.

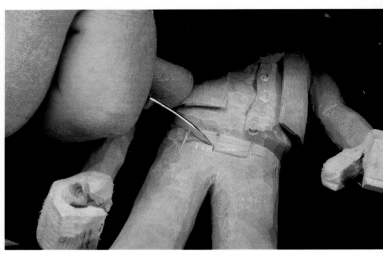

Put a stop cut along the side of the belt buckle and under the belt, intersecting with the side of the belt buckle.

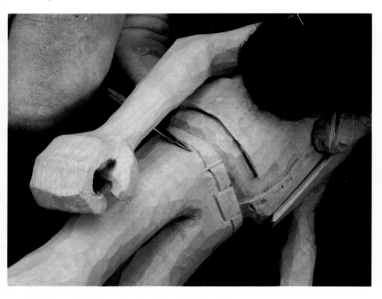

Relieve the belt on both sides of the belt loop.

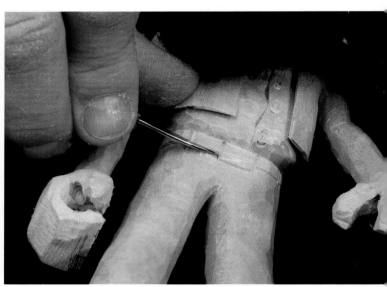

Flick out the triangle of wood at this intersection of the belt and buckle.

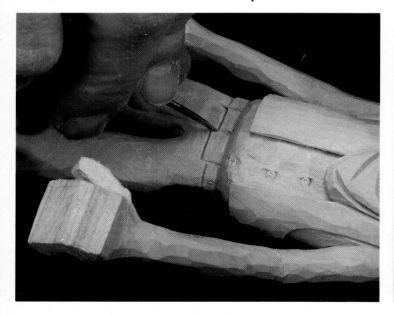

Relieve the pant to the bottom of the belt.

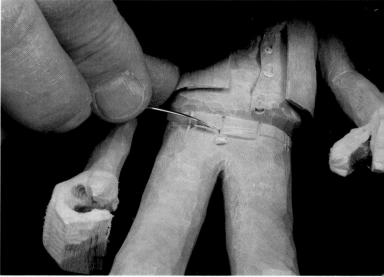

Relieve the belt buckle and the belt.

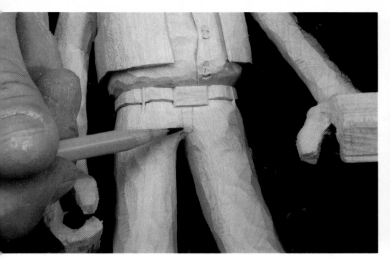

Draw in the fly.

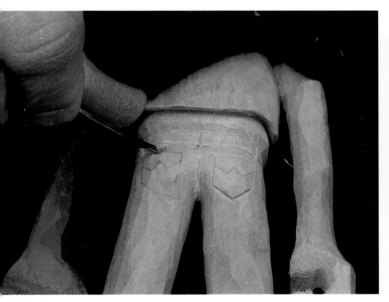

The rear pockets are drawn in with a pencil. Use the small V tool to outline both pockets ...

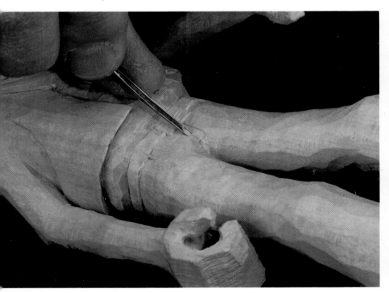

... and the fly.

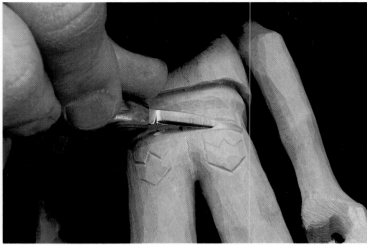

Using the detail knife, relieve the wood around the pockets. Notice the Wrangler stitching on the back pockets. I use Wrangler jeans because most cowboys use them.

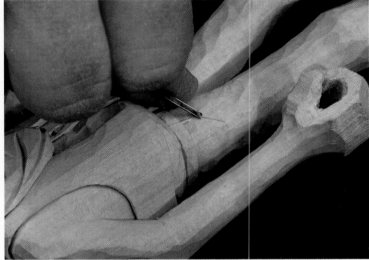

Use the V tool to indicate the openings of the front pockets.

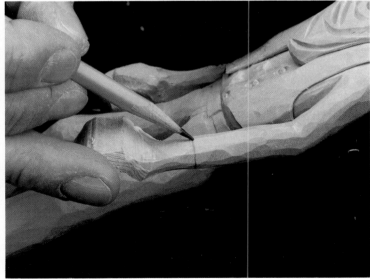

Well, we've saved the hardest part for next to last. First locate the top of the shirt cuff on each arm.

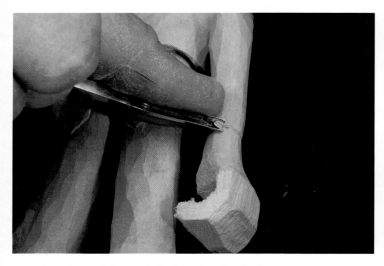

Follow that cuff line with the 1/8" V tool on both arms.

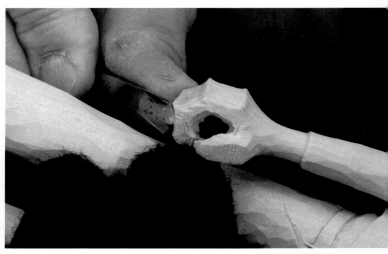

Proceed on down the hand, removing saw marks. The objective is to keep the knuckles raised above the fingers. Make the cuts in such a way that the knuckles are pronounced.

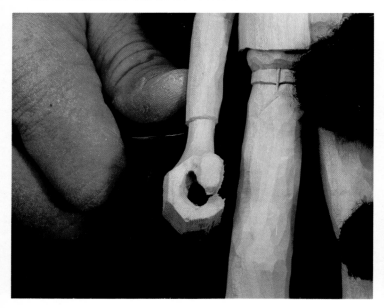

Beginning with your cuts on the hand, relieve the arm to the top of the shirt cuff with a bench knife. Try to keep this section of the arm cylindrical.

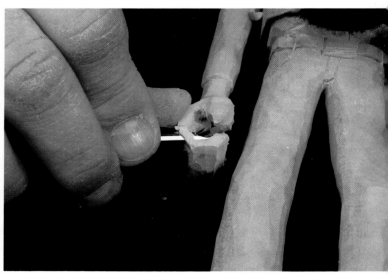

Gently remove the saw marks from the tops of the knuckles with the detail knife. Remove saw marks from front and rear of the fingers as well.

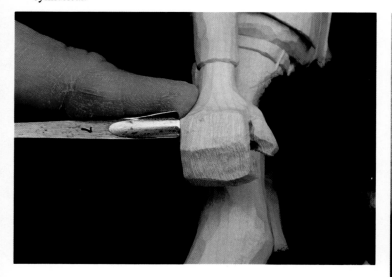

With your 1/2" #7 gouge, remove saw marks between the knuckles as shown.

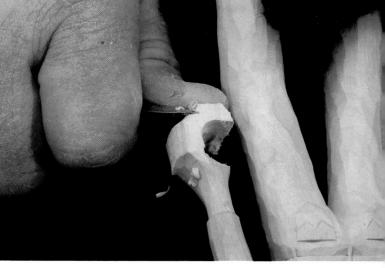

Then round the fingers.

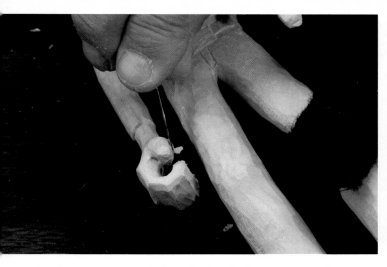

Gently remove saw marks from the thumb, shape to your preference while accenting the arthritic knuckles.

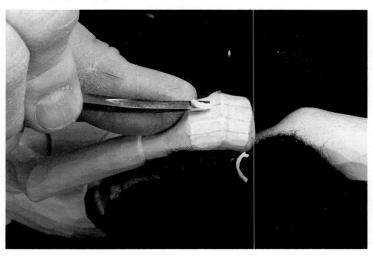

To carve in the fingers, first sketch with a pencil, then cut out along the lines with the medium V tool.

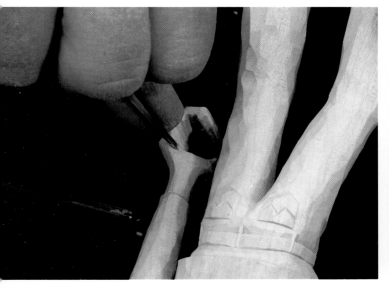

Use small gouges to remove wood from the inside of the hand and the backside of the thumb. Be patient, it takes time to remove the excess wood from this fragile area.

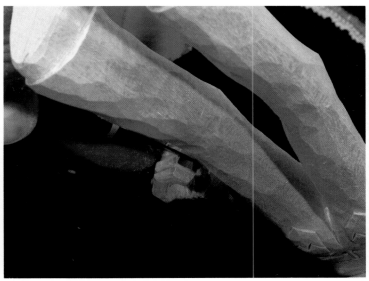

Use tip of detail knife to reach tight spots.

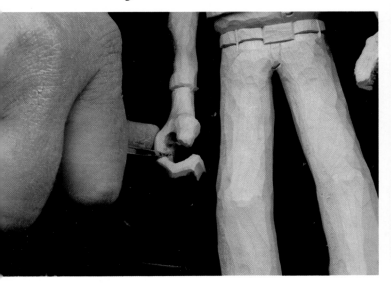

Round the inside of fingers with a detail knife.

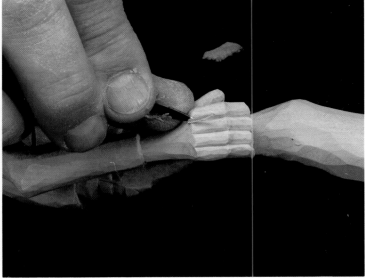

Use detail knife to round fingers and to accent the space between fingers.

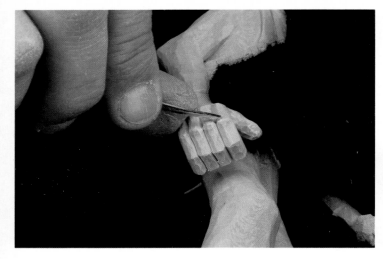

Define folds and loose skin around the knuckles with the detail knife

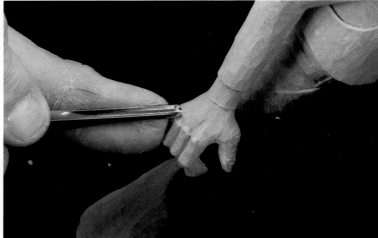

Use 3/16" deep gouge to indicate ligaments between upper finger joints.

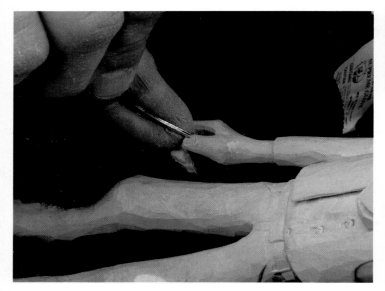

... and to outline thumb nails and fingernails where wanted or possible to place.

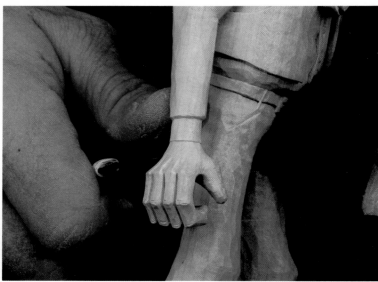

Congratulations, there's the completed hand.

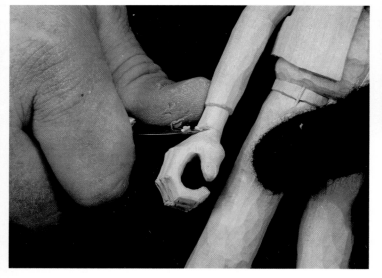

Score a very shallow cut along the bottom of the shirt cuff. Relieve the hand to bottom of this shallow cut with the detail knife as well.

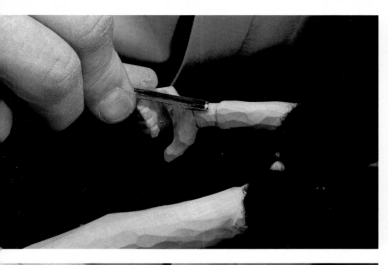

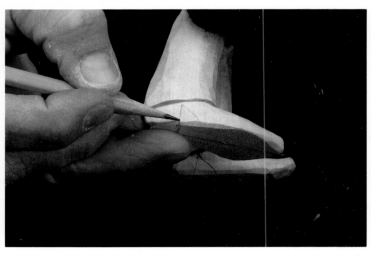

To detail the boot, start by drawing in the heel of the boot.

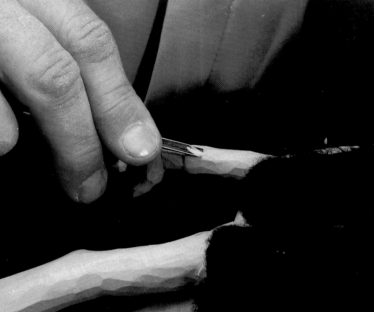

One last detail on the shirt cuff. Form the overlap of the cuff and the placket above the cuff by laying your V tool on one edge and cutting a straight line to the top of the cuff. Turn the V tool upright and continue the cut of the placket into the shirt sleeve.

Using a large V tool cut in the heel.

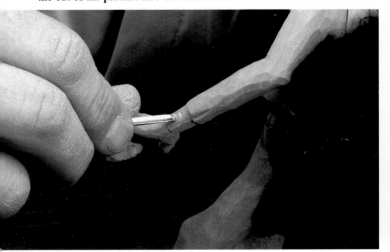

Finally, we will form a button on the cuff using the same technique as was used on the shirt front.

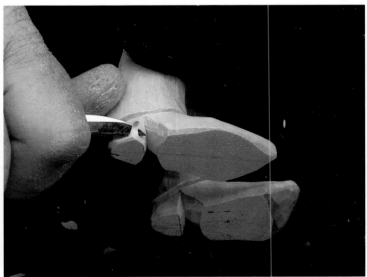

Deepen this cut and to round the heel with your bench knife.

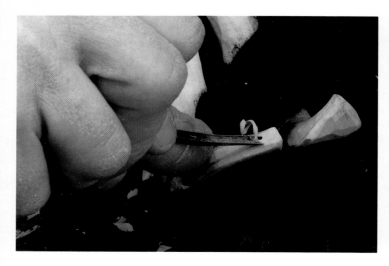

Sketch in the line of the boot sole. Use the medium V tool to outline the sole.

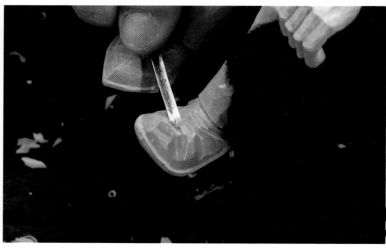

With a combination of the bench knife, deep gouges and V tools, age and give character to the boots.

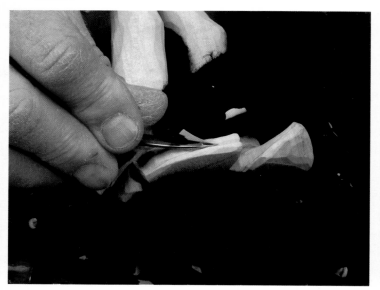

Use your bench knife to relieve the boot from the top of the sole ...

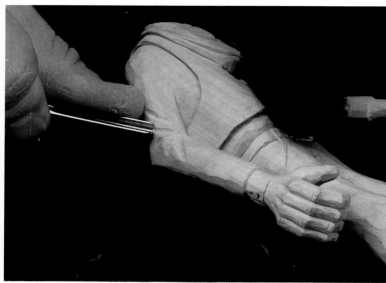

The last thing we want to do to complete the detailing of the body is to add creases and folds in the shirt and pants legs. I use a combination of deep gouges, V tools and a bench knife to cut these folds in. The folds at articulation points radiate from those points.

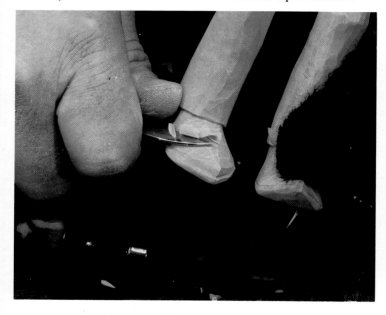

... and round the top part of the boot.

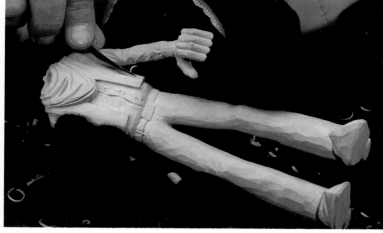

Since we twisted this vest to keep all of our lines from following the center line of the body, we will need to indicate some folds along the left side of the vest.

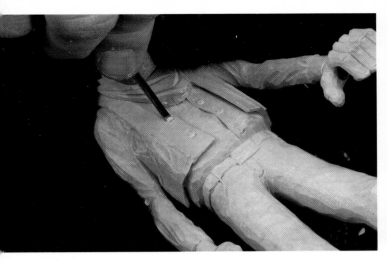

Add a few buttons to the vest.

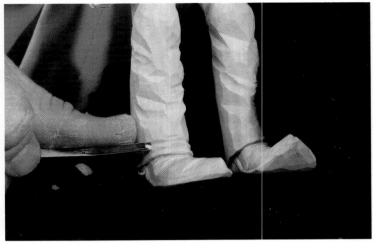

Indicate the bunched up lower leading edge of the pants leg with a V tool.

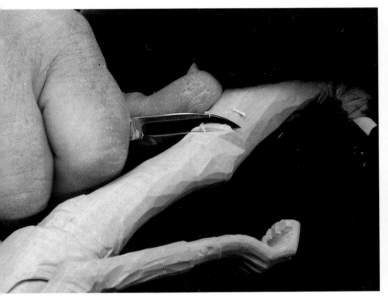

Start with some rather bold cuts in the pant legs with the bench knife.

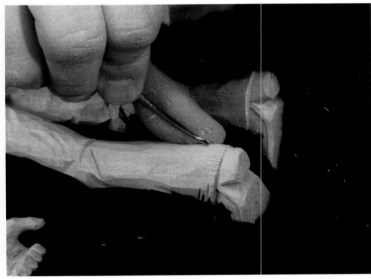

Depict the frayed rear portion of the pants leg with a small V tool.

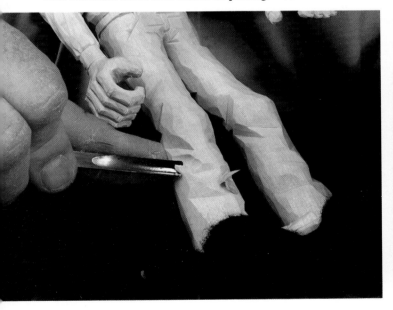

Use gouges to add to these bold knife cuts.

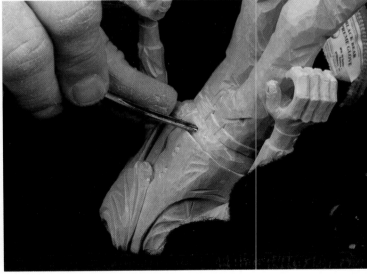

Use the small V tool to indicate folds in the shirt where it is tucked into the pants as well.

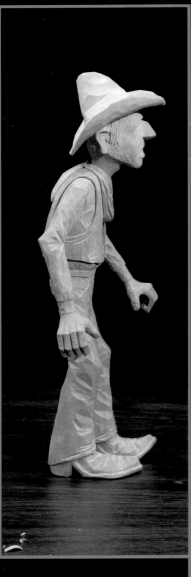
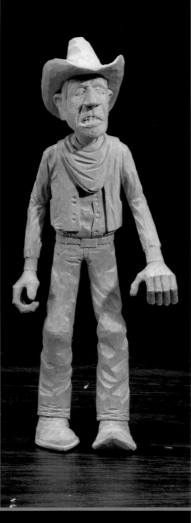

Here is what this old guy looks like after the carving is completed.

PAINTING THE COWBOY

Painting: At various times in my carving career, I have used water colors, straight acrylics and oils. I prefer Ceramcoat pre-mixed acrylics by Delta. There are other brands of these pre-mixed colors on the market but Ceramcoat has the best selection and the most consistent colors. Except for eyes, buttons, belt buckle and occasionally other small details, I make a wash of colors, mixing them with water. To keep colors from running together on the cowboys, I try not to paint contiguous surfaces until one is dry. You can speed up this process by using a hand held hair dryer.

I don't use the best quality or most expensive brushes on the market. I elect to use medium quality brushes, wear them out and buy new ones. I do this because I like to buy new things to play with. The more gadgets and toys the better. The colors I use most often for the various parts of the cowboy are:

Flesh: Caucasian Flesh #2029 and medium Flesh #2126.
Jeans: Midnight Blue #2114.
Boots, Vest, Belts, Hats and other leather: Brown Iron Oxide #2023, Burnt Umber #2025, Territorial Beige #2025 and Black (no number).
Button snaps and other metal: Silver #6003 and Gold #6002.
Bandanna: Fire Red #2083.
Eyes: White (no number), Blue Haze #2122 or Avalon #2417.
Hair: Drizzle Grey #2452, Brown Iron Oxide #2023, Burnt Umber #2025, Territorial Beige #2425, Black (no number).
Shirts: Purple #2091, Laguna #2418, Grape #2048, Ocean Reef #2074, Pumpkin #2042, Fiesta Pink #2045, Orange #2026, Yellow #2504, Iron Oxide #2020, Drizzle Grey #2452, Turquoise #2012 and others as desired.

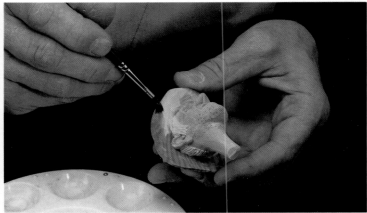

First use 3 parts of Caucasian Flesh and about 1 part medium Flesh mixed with 4 parts water. Mix well with a brush before applying. Paint the head using a #2 brush, being careful not to get paint on the hat or hair. Make sure you paint over the inside of the mouth including the teeth and the eyeballs with this flesh color because we will cover these later with undiluted white. Some carvers do not like to paint their own carvings but I encourage you to try because you will become a better carver as a result of painting your own work. Paint the hands and any other exposed flesh with the same flesh mixture.

To paint the jeans apply 1 part Midnight Blue and 4 parts water with a little bit larger brush for the jeans and other large feature. This is a #4 brush. Don't forget the belt loops.

Mix 1 part Brown Iron Oxide with 4 parts water. Paint the hat using the #2 brush. There are a couple advantages to using water in the paint: you use smaller amounts of your expensive paints every time, the wood grain will show through the paint which warms the figure, and the water will cause the wood to expand. When the wood expands, any unwanted cuts made by an unplanned slip of the knife will close.

Use the same brown mixture on the boots, vest and belt.

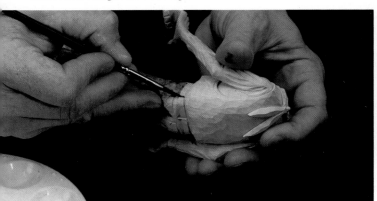

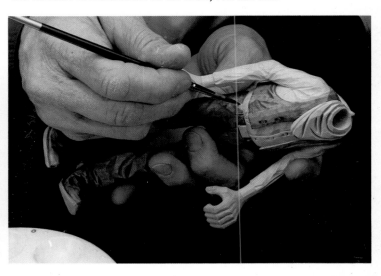

Paint the eyeballs and teeth with undiluted white.

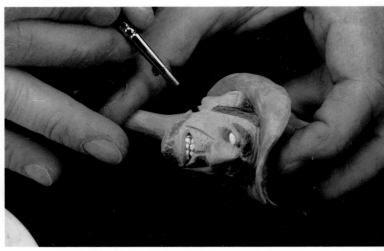

Dry brush this diluted black over the beard stubble as well.

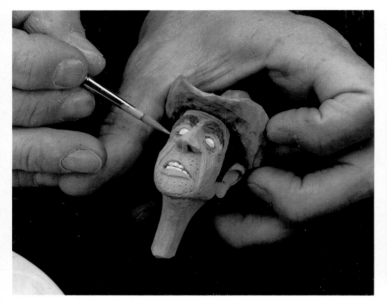

Now mix 1 part black with 8 parts water to paint the hair with a #4 brush. Continue to the eyebrows and the bags under the eyes with the hair color as well, toning down the bags with some of the mixed flesh color.

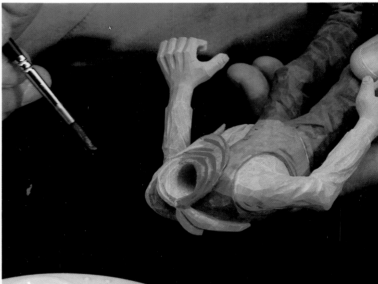

Let's paint our bandanna now. Mix 1 part Fire Red with 4 parts water and apply with a #4 brush.

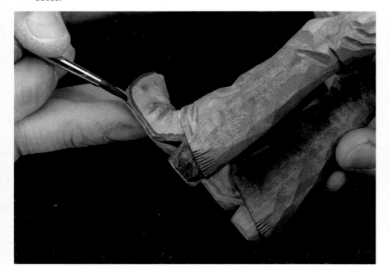

Use the same black mix to paint the soles of the boots.

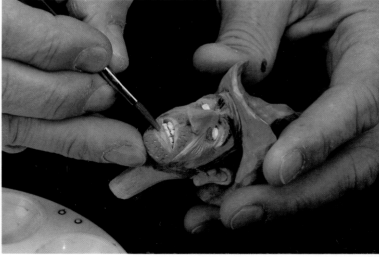

Mix the diluted red with a little bit of the flesh tone and highlight the cheeks, the nose and the top of the ears of the cowboy to indicate a little sunburn.

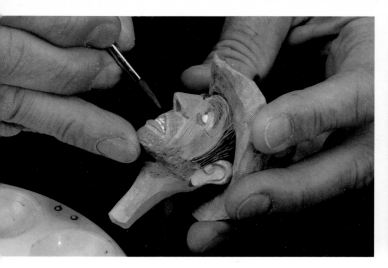

To that mixture add a little more red to outline the lips ...

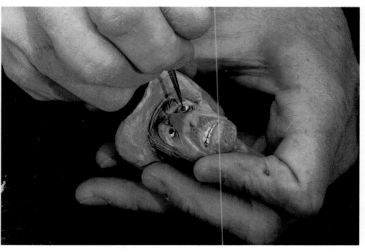

Use undiluted black and the .50 brush to apply the pupils to the eyes once each iris dries.

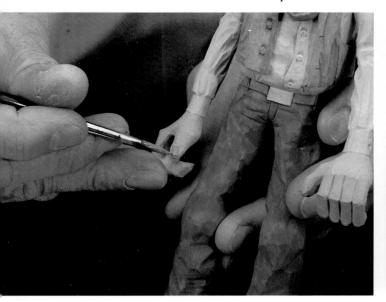

... and paint the finger nails.

Mix 4 parts water and 1 part Purple to paint the shirt with a #4 brush.

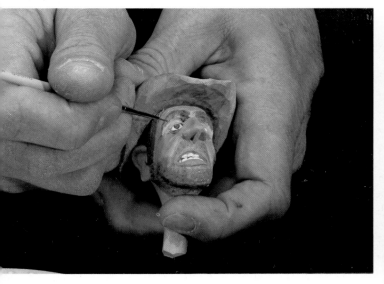

Paint in the iris of the eyes with undiluted Avalon with a .50 brush (very small). Since we have carved this cowboy with an expression of irritation, we should paint the iris up towards the upper lid.

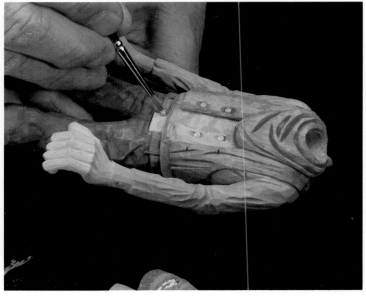

We use undiluted Silver to paint the belt buckle and buttons.

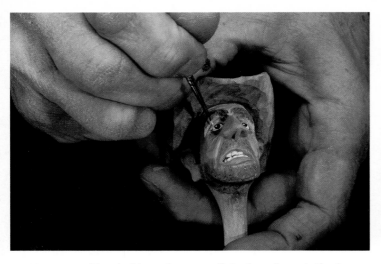

Now use undiluted white and put a small dot in each eye indicating light reflecting on the cornea.

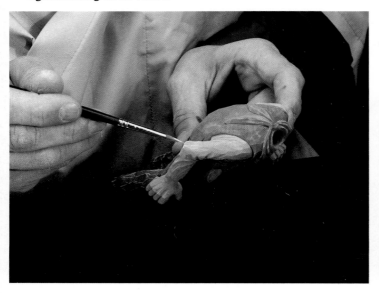

Dry brush over the jeans and shirt elbows with a #4 brush and undiluted white paint to indicate age and general wear-and-tear.

Dry brush white into the hair as well, showing age and personal wear-and-tear.

The next step is designed to do four things: 1. it seals the wood, 2. it tones down the harshness of the acrylic colors, 3. it antiques the character by collecting in the undercuts and other nooks-and-crannies, and 4. it hides minor mistakes in the paint. It is a mixture of about 10 parts boiled Linseed oil and 1 part dark walnut Minwax stain. Brush this mixture onto the carving.

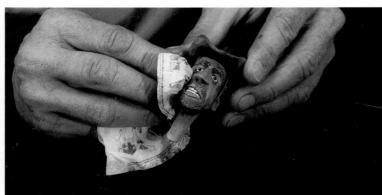

Wipe off the excess Linseed oil mixture with a soft cloth or super-absorbent paper towel and allow to dry about 24 hours before applying the finishing coat of semigloss Verathane 2001. For a more intense antique look, do not wipe as carefully. Linseed oil has a tendency to spontaneously combust so it is advisable to keep the rags in an airtight container until they can be properly disposed of.

Verathane 2001 is a water soluble semigloss finishing glaze. However, heavy coats or more than one thin coat will cause the cowboy to be somewhat glossy. Apply with an old, cheap #6 brush. Apply sparingly and brush until milky appearance disappears.

The completed cowboy. All you cowgirls out there, check out the tight jeans and these tight little buns.

THE GALLERY

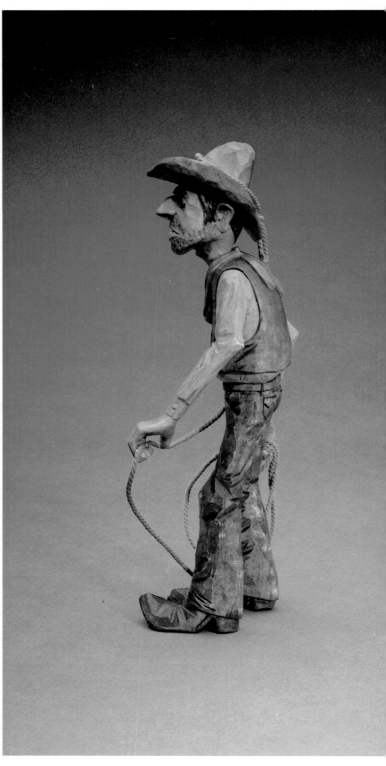

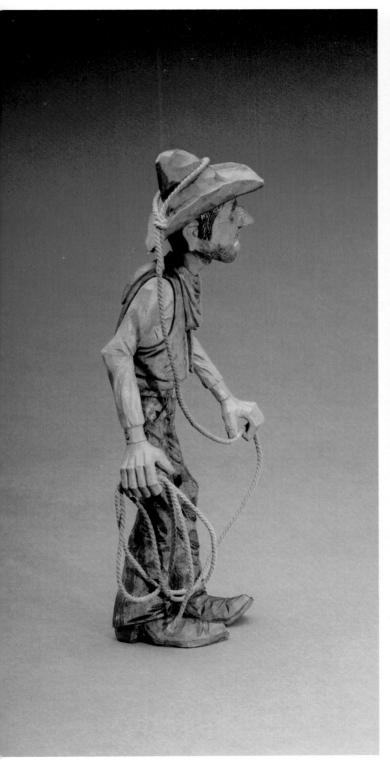

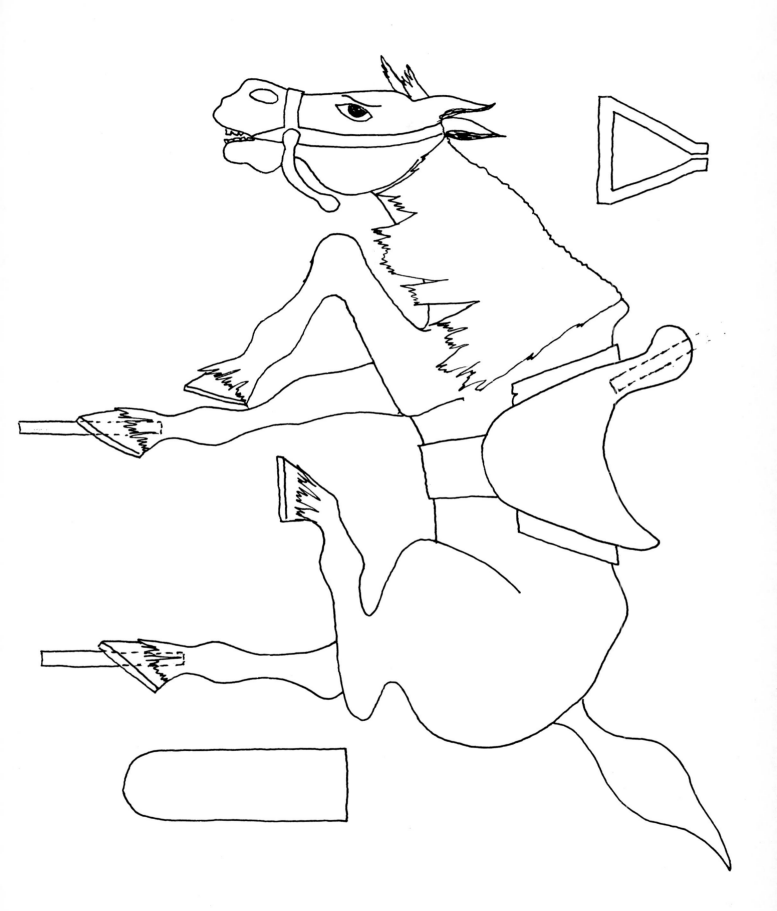